U H University of Hertfordshire

College Lane, Hatfield, Herts. AL10 9AB

Learning and Information Services

For renewal of Standard and One Week Loans,
please visit the web site **http://www.voyager.herts.ac.uk**

This item must be returned or the loan renewed by the due date.
The University reserves the right to recall items from loan at any time.
A fine will be charged for late return of items.

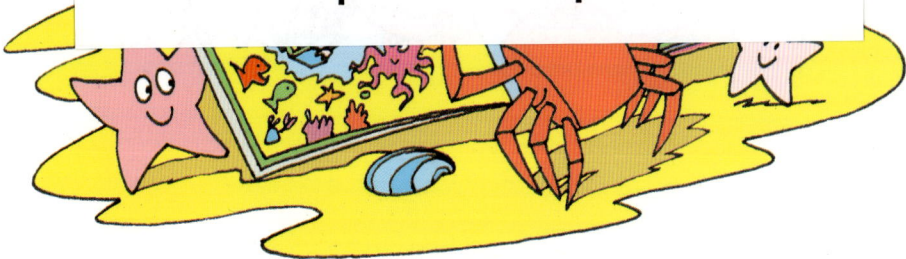

PONT *poetry*

First impression – 2004

ISBN 1 84323 344 4

© poems: the poets
© illustrations: Chris Glynn

This book is also available in Big Book format
(ISBN 1 84323 345 2)

Printed in Wales at
Gomer Press, Llandysul, Ceredigion SA44 4JL
www.gomer.co.uk

Contents

Swimming with the Fishes

In my wet suit and my flippers
with a breathing tube and mask,

I'd go swimming with the fishes
and I know what I would ask.

Does a starfish shine at night
when it's lying on the sands?

Can an octopus count to ten
with eight tentacles but no hands?

What makes a jellyfish wobble?
What shocks an electric eel?

And why do crabs crab sideways?
Are mermaids really real?

Neil Nuttall

The Seasons

When spring arrives I'm happy,
I sing and play and shout.
All day the sun shines brightly,
At night the moon comes out.

Now summer's here, we're on the beach,
The sun, the sand, iced lollies.
But just in case it starts to rain
Mum always takes our brollies.

In autumn I go walking
On carpets of brown leaves.
They lie like scraps of paper
Beneath the tall, bare trees.

But best of all there's winter.
I come in from the snow.
I snuggle on the sofa
My face and feet aglow.

Phil Carradice

It's a Wonderful Life

At the bottom of the garden
A snail has made his home,
Sometimes friends come visiting,
So he is not alone.

The grass is green and lovely,
The flowers pink and yellow,
It's absolutely perfect!
That snail's a lucky fellow.

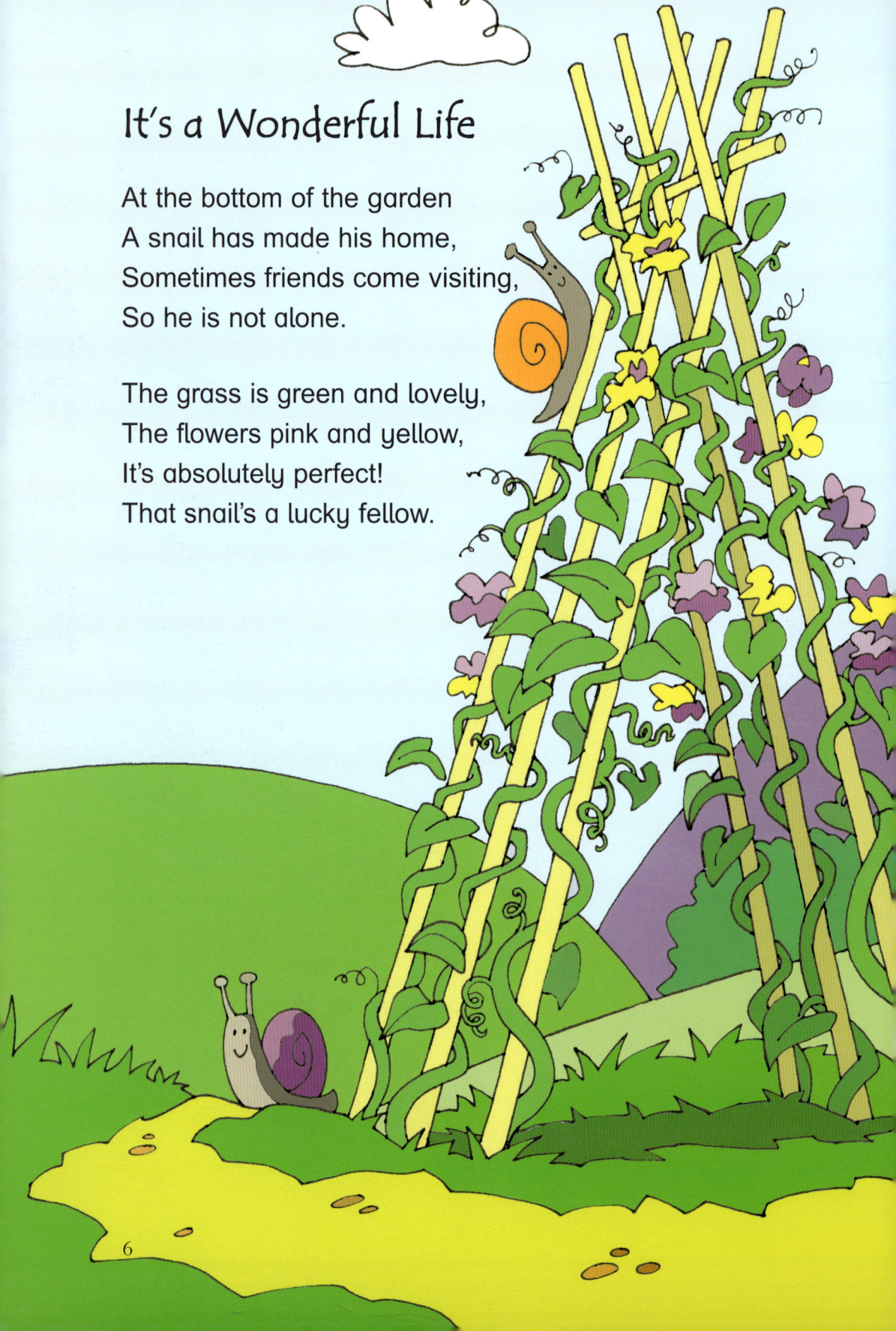

Underneath a rhubarb leaf
He has a dozy time,
Lying in a spiral bath,
While his clothes dry on the line.

No-one in the village
Knows that he is there,
That happy dozy spiral snail,
Living without a care.

Francesca Kay

On My Way to School

Up the road and round the corner
On my way to school
I met the fire-breathing dragon
That heats the swimming pool.

Up the road and down the hill
On my way to school
I met the ghost who makes doors slam
And always plays the fool

Up the road, across the bridge
On my way to school
I met the giant who eats huge sweets
And that was really cool.

Helen Woods

Seaside Gale

Look at the boat,
in the seaside gale,
play hide and seek
as the white gulls sail
through the rainbow sky
and windy waves
crash lighthouse-high.

Hold on to the dog!
Hold on to the rail!
Hold on to the baby
in a seaside gale!

Neil Nuttall

9

Trolley Dash

Just enough time
To do the shopping
Before the match begins.
Dad's in a sweat –
He's lost Mum's list
And what if Wales don't win?

'Come on, Dad,
Push a bit harder,
No time to relax!'
Grab some pop,
Chicken crunchies,
Beer and crisps and snacks.

'Come on, Dad,
Frozen chips this way!'
Dashing down the aisles.
Our hearts sink
As we reach the checkout –
The queue goes on for miles!

Back in the car,
The list's on the dashboard,
Dad begins to read:
'Apples, oranges,
Cabbage, stir-fry . . .'
Healthy foods we need . . .

Ooops!

Ruth Morgan

Magic Feet

Once my little feet
helped me wheel
up our street
my dad's barrow
or baby's pushchair.
One day, if I try,
and I've wings
I may fly;
then I'll soar like
a bird in the air.
But my MAGIC FEET
take me out
of our street,
today when I roar
like a bike.
As I speed off – you bet
I'm as fast as a jet;
I may race like a car,
or zoom to a star.

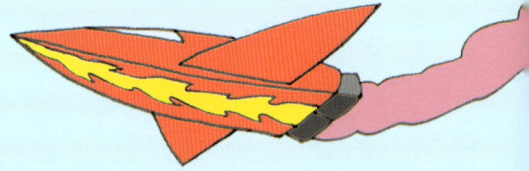

I can fly
with the sound
of a plane
looping round;
or pogo and bound
with a stick
on the ground.
My feet can go slow
if I paddle or row
my canoe on the seas
or a pond.
And I've chugged
up and down
ploughing fields
green and brown
over all of our street
and beyond!

Neil Nuttall

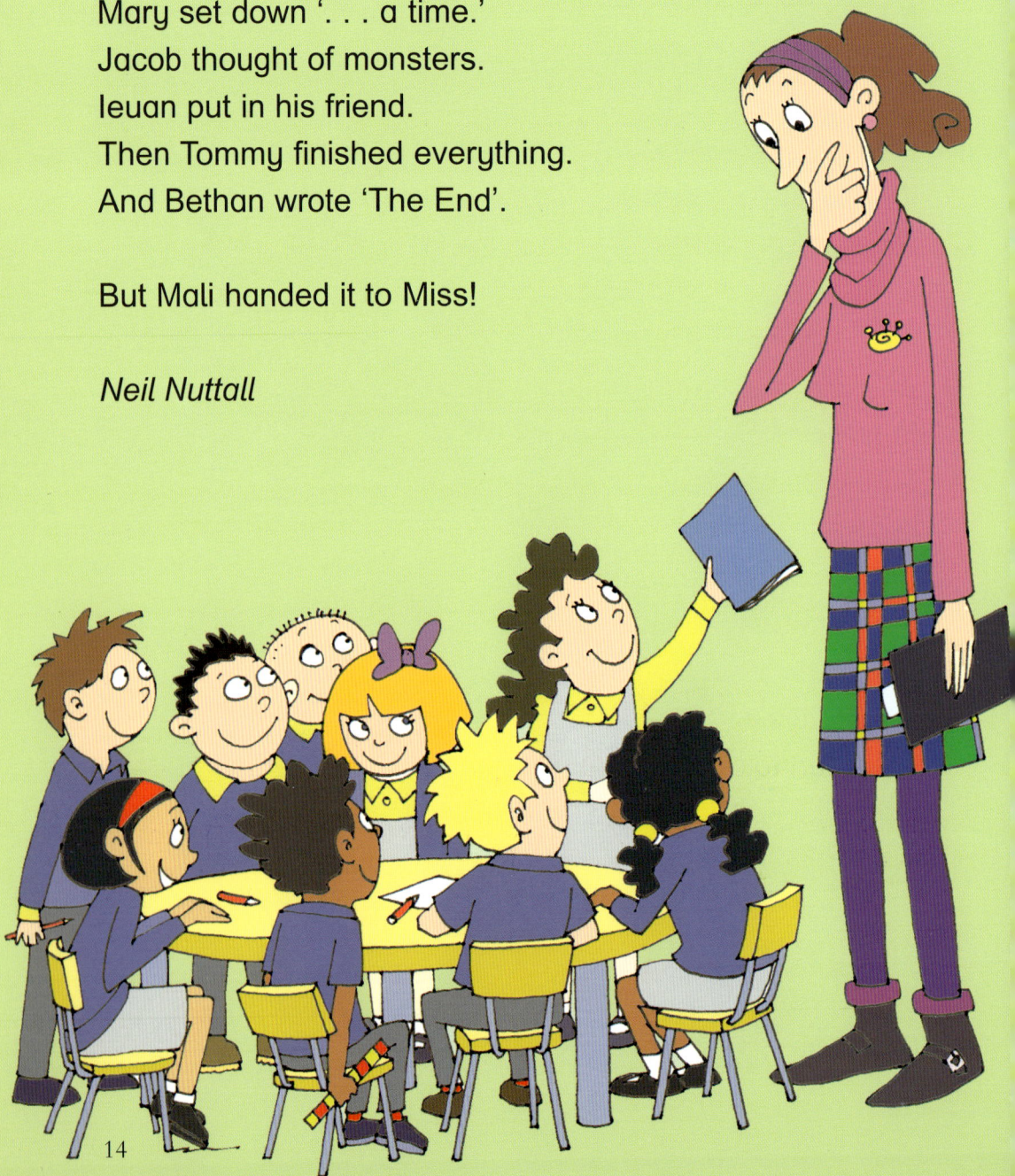

Mali's Story

Carly chose the title.
Rhys did the underline.
Gwyn wrote the 'Once upon . . .'
Mary set down '. . . a time.'
Jacob thought of monsters.
Ieuan put in his friend.
Then Tommy finished everything.
And Bethan wrote 'The End'.

But Mali handed it to Miss!

Neil Nuttall

My Voice

I can make a sound
When I use my voice,
I can shout and scream
For my favourite team.

I can bawl and cry,
I can make a noise
When I've fallen down,
Or I've lost my toy.

I can jabber and babble
And talk all day,
In the street or on the 'phone.

I can sing a song
At the top of my voice
In a crowd or all alone.

But there's just one sound
I've been told I make
That I've never heard before:
When I'm flat worn out
At the end of the day
And I fall asleep and *snore*!

Ruth Morgan

Martin's Mood

'Martin, darling, have some pie.'
'I'm not hungry!' comes the cry.
'We've cut your fishcakes into stars.'
'You can send them up to Mars!'

'You used to love sprouts such a lot.'
'I did not, not, not, not, NOT!'

'How about some pasta bows?'
'Go and stick them up your nose.'

Dear Martin purses up his lips
To make sure not a spoonful past them slips.

Mum cuts a piece of cherry pie.
She's going to give it one last try.

What a mistake!

'DON'T WANT TO!
NOT GOING TO!
WON'T HAVE IT!
DON'T LIKE IT!
I'LL THROW IT . . . see?'

Mealtimes are a battle
When Martin's in a mood.
Why don't they just let him be
When he won't eat his food?

Ruth Morgan

The Grumble Rumble

There's a rolling, echoey
Rumbling sound
Down in my insides,
My Grumble Rumble's woken up
And I can hear his cries:

'Feed me chips!
Nuggets, dips!
Strawberry milkshake first!
I want to chew and scoff and chomp
Until I'm fit to burst!'

There's a jumpy,
Grumpy feeling
Deep inside as well.
My Grumble Rumble's getting mad
And now he starts to yell:

'Beans on toast!
Sunday Roast!
Swill it down with pop!
I want to chew and scoff and chomp
And never, ever stop!'

Ruth Morgan

Piggy Wiggy

They think it's very funny
That I really love my money
But it isn't really money
That I love.

My Piggy Wiggy's greedy
And for money he is needy
So it's money that I feed the
Pig I love.

Helen Woods

Money for Old Teeth

My little baby teeth fell out,
My mouth was pink and gummy,
Then fairies took the teeth away,
And left me lots of money!

Francesca Kay

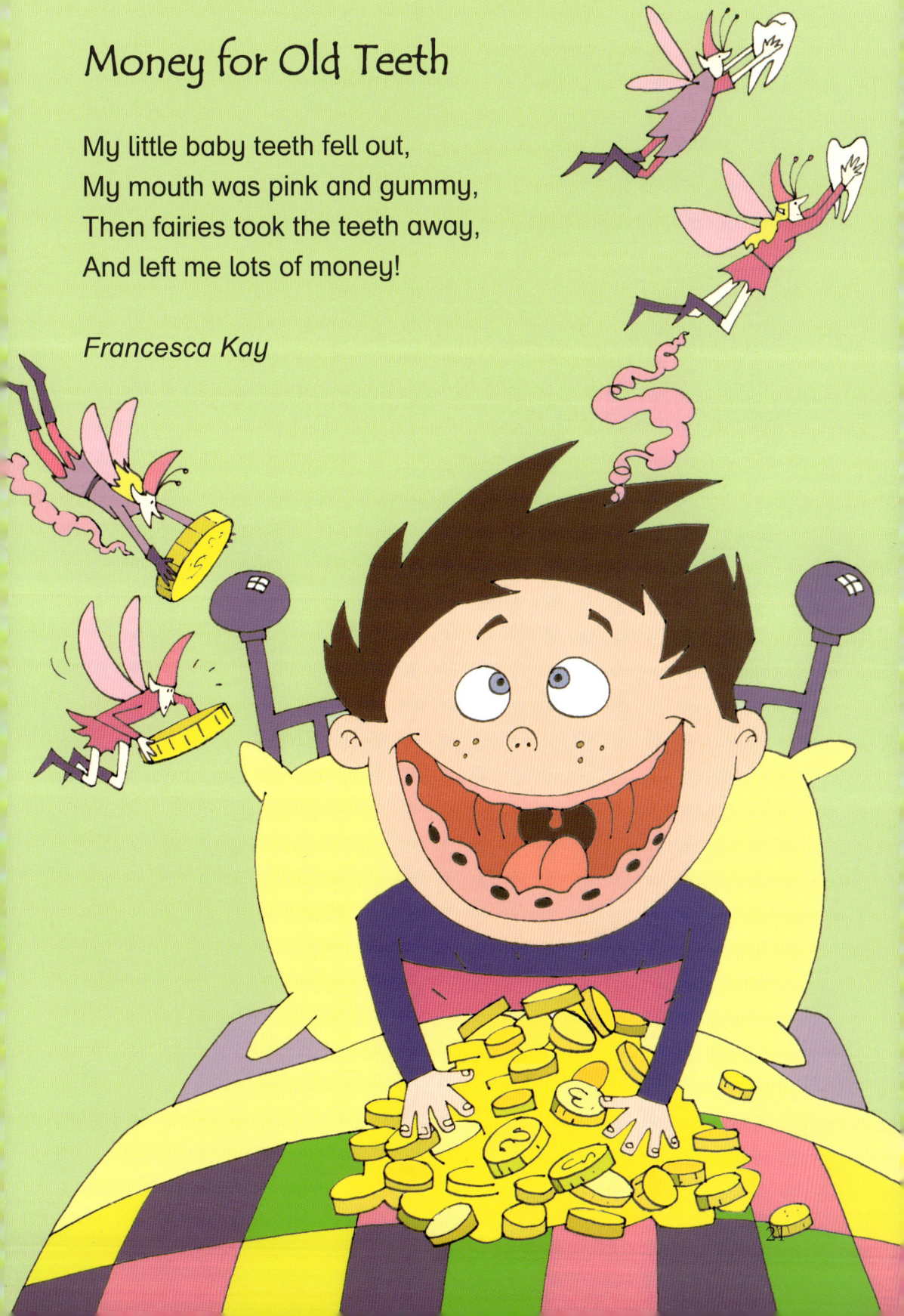

Making Mischief

We're the weather workers,
Little mischief makers,
We're the snowy sprinklers,
And the wailing winds.

We're the frosty freezers,
Running over rainbows,
And on our cheeky faces,
You'll see great big grins.

We're the cloud collectors,
Super sunshine splashers,
We love making weather,
Dashing everywhere.

Running in the rainclouds,
Hurtling through the hailstones,
Wherever you find weather,
We are always there.

Perhaps one day you'll see us,
On the misty mountain,
Whistling with the whirling wind,
Or shining in the sun.

Making all your weather,
We are always busy,
Yes, we're the mischief makers,
Having such a lot of fun!

Francesca Kay

That's What You Get!

Under the table
And then up the stairs,
Over the sideboard,
Across all the chairs.

Melanie's shouting,
Tony stops, quick,
Leroy is rapping,
Chelsea feels sick.

The cat's in the kitchen,
He's chasing a mouse.
There's shouting and screaming
All over the house.

There's balls in the hallway
And toys on the table,
There's cake on the carpet
And Ali's pinched Mabel.

"Make sure you behave,"
Our mums and dads say.
They don't understand –
It's a party today.

We're running like demons,
So fit and so sporty.
Our parents should know,
We don't try to be naughty.

It sort of, like, happens,
It's gone on for ever,
But that's what you get
When you put kids together!

Phil Carradice

Waiting for Mr Green

We all lined up to cross the road
And waited while the Red Man showed.
He watched us with his eyes unblinking,
Each of us knew what he was thinking –
'Wait here until the road is clear,
In time the Green Man will appear.
Then follow him across the street
In one straight line, all nice and neat.'

The Green Man came, we hurried on
And listened to his warning song –
'Don't cross the road until I'm here.
Just wait for me, I'm always near.
Make sure you walk where you'll be seen
And always, always cross on green.'
We'll always remember what the two of them said –
The kind, wise words of Mr Green and Red.

Phil Carradice

Shh . . .

It's late at night,
They're all asleep.
Don't make a sound,
Not a scratch, not a peep.

Where have you been
So late at night?
Look at your paws –
Did you climb, did you fight?

Who did you see,
My smiling cat?
Did you meet friends
Or a bird, or a rat?

Who's that up there
At such a height?
Looks like a witch
On a trip, on a flight.

Helen Woods

The Wild Wind

On the hills outside town
A wild wind is blowing
But whether she's angry
There's no way of knowing.

She whistles, she roars,
Then puffs out her face
And glares at the fields
Where Patch and I race.

The wind is so cold,
She sings in loud notes,
But Patch and I smile
In our warm winter coats.

Phil Carradice

I've Been Busy

Look here, Mr Sun,
See what I can do!
With my paintbrush I've changed everything,
I've even painted you!

What do you think of your purple face,
With the orange sky around,
And the mountains like a rainbow,
Spread out on the ground?

Do you want to shine down on the trees,
With their glossy leaves of pink?
And look at my pet piggy,
All green – what do you think?

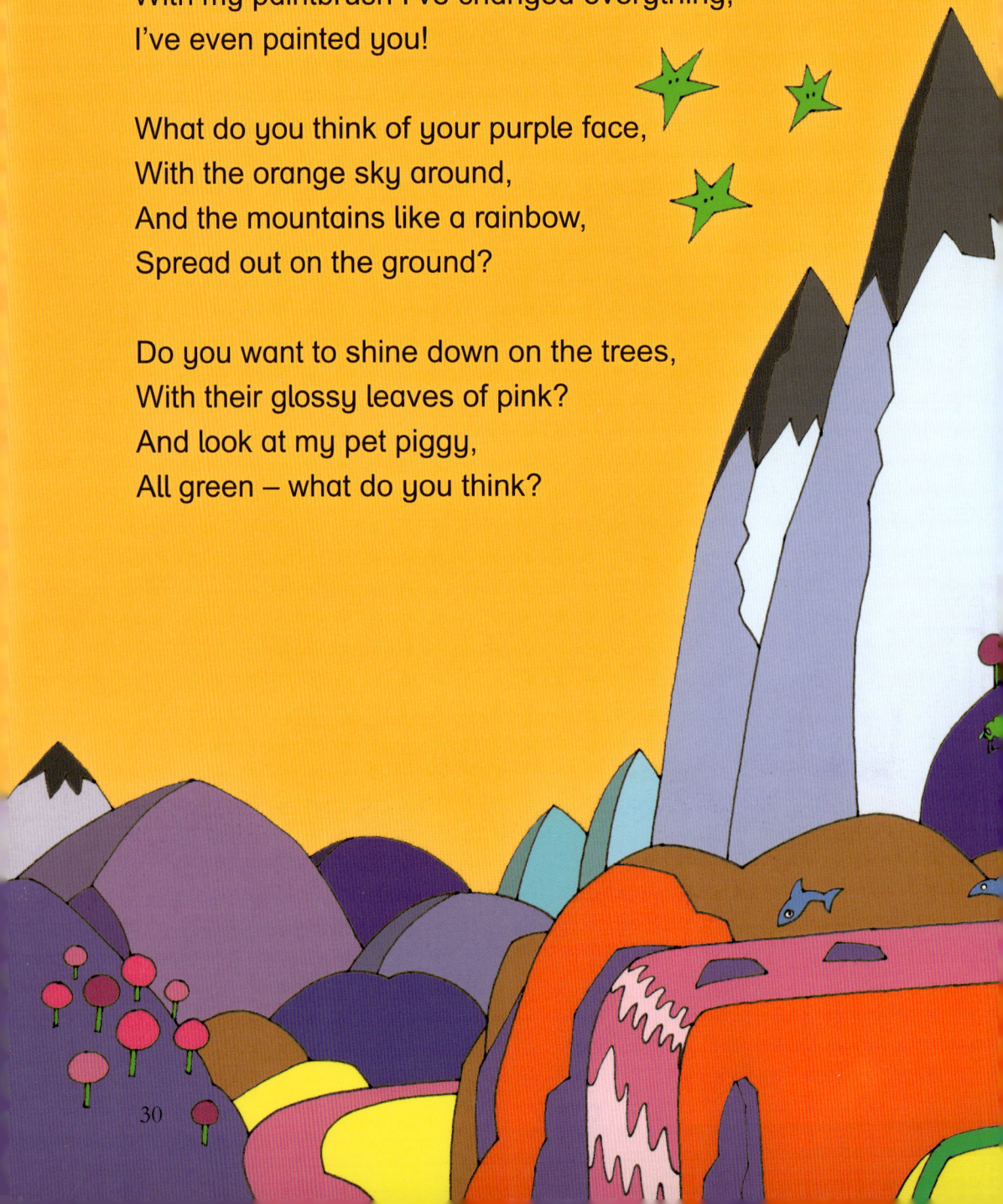

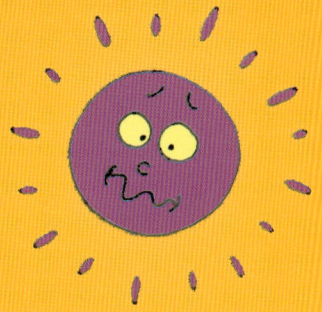

I'm such a happy artist,
I've been painting all the day,
Now the world is different –
Mr Sun, what do you say?

If you don't like it, Mr Sun,
And want the old colours back again,
We'll need to wash the paint right off,
So let's wait for Mr Rain!

Francesca Kay

31

What Have You Got?

What have you got?
Can I see?
Is it something good to eat
And will you share with me?

What have you got?
Can I touch?
Is it a baby dinosaur
You love so very much?

What have you got
In your hand?
Is it teeny tiny folk
As small as grains of sand?

What have you got?
Please show me.
Is it special little seeds
To grow a magic tree?

What have you got?
Tell us, do!
Did you kiss your hand and make
 A wish you hope comes true?

Helen Woods